RAND PAUL VS TED CRUZ 2016

The Libertarian-Conservative GOP Primary Battle
for the Soul of the Republican Party

by

Trevor Smith

Rand Paul vs. Ted Cruz
2016

The Libertarian-Conservative GOP Primary Battle For the Soul of the Republican Party

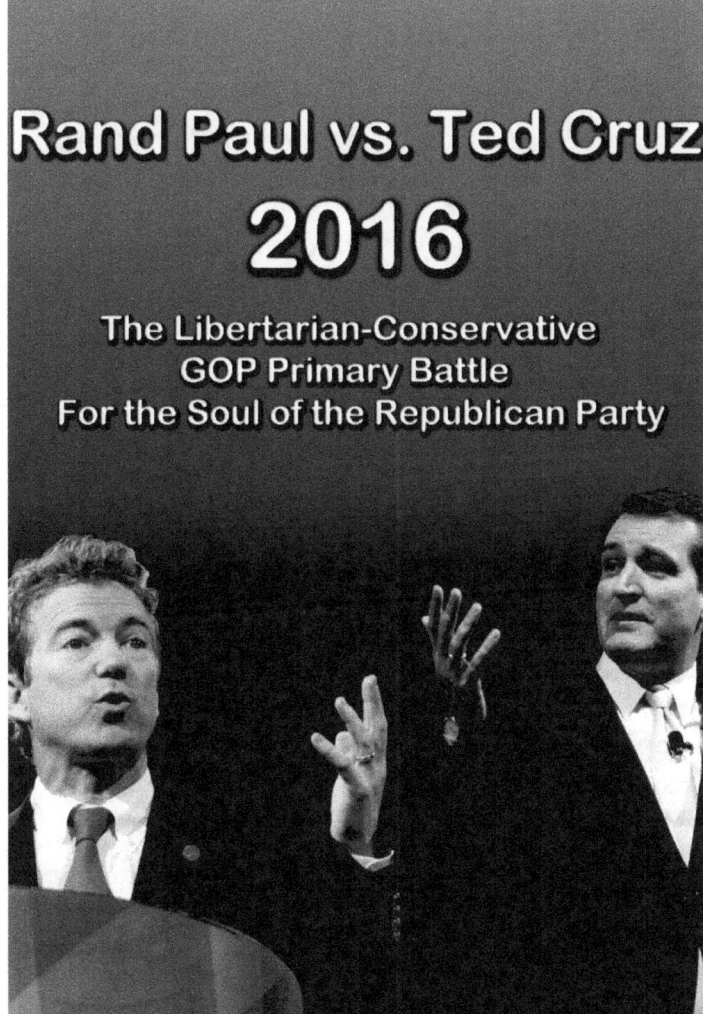

Cover photos from professional photographer
Gage Skidmore

For hire at GageSkidmore.com

©2015 Reactionary Press

Contents

Dedicated to Mary Ann.
You will always be missed.

You loved to read and loved to laugh.
You loved liberty and loved life.

Preface: Unity or Principle?

The GOP is in the midst of a struggle. Throughout the beginning of the 21st century, the beginning shots of this new "civil war" rang out as a clear clarion call. Most of the media claims this is a battle between "social conservatives" and "libertarians".

For some, however, there is not just one struggle, but two struggles. It is probably undeniable that there is a battle between these two ideological wings of the party, but there is an even bigger battle raging: between the "grassroots" and the "establishment".

Before we delve into what libertarians and social conservatives believe, how they differ, and so forth, we must come to the agreement that having people of principle in our party is generally a good thing. But when those principles differ it can lead to division. In truth, more principle only unites us, it doesn't divide.

Yet there is a group of people in our party who disagree with even the idea of having principles, shockingly. These people are the "establishment" Republicans, often labeled RINOs (Republicans in Name Only). To these "elitist" individuals, they believe incorrectly that compromise is what wins elections, so they compromise on their values in order to get the reins of power.

To a small degree, compromise can be a good thing, but the establishment GOP do it to such an extent that principle no longer exists, and power is the only objective.

They morph into the very enemy they are elected to fight, the progressives, in order to "beat" them. But by doing so, they have essentially become "Progressive lite", a watered down version of the enemy's policies. It is as if they have taken the saying "If you can't beat 'em, join 'em" as their political mantra.

Beyond simple compromise, the Establishment GOP often outright conspire with the enemy: in Texas, the current Speaker of the House, Joe Straus, actually overthrew the more conservative Speaker, Tom Craddick, using mostly Democratic votes for him as Speaker and hardly any GOP votes.

So the GOP in Texas was defeated by the Democrats with the help of a few RINO traitors backstabbing them. Recently the principled black conservative Scott Turner attempted to unseat Straus, but only garnered a handful of votes from Tea Party backed candidates, while GOP Speaker Joe Straus got 100% of the Democrat vote, allied with the RINO vote. Similar events happen all across America.

Worth noting, Jeff Judson (JeffJudson.com) is now running against Straus to take out this RINO traitor. Straus is "the last roadblock for effecting true change in Texas", according to the Tea Party. Texas allows out-of-state donors, so please donate if you can, he needs help!

With such traitors like Straus in our midst openly allying themselves with the enemy Democrats, principled people like the Libertarians can be a welcome ally for Conservatives fighting against this treachery.

The establishment has recently understood it's own vulnerability and has been calling for "party unity" at most state conventions. This is a way of trying to silence the people who are booing the RINOs at the state conventions, and to discourage conservatives from stopping the elitists by censuring RINOs at the convention.

John McCain, for example, was censured in Arizona by the GOP. This was a slap to his face to say that basically he has betrayed the party. Unfortunately, the GOP convention did not remove his party credentials. Many of even the most dedicated conservative activists do not understand the party rules or analyze it to find ways to attack at the corruption festering inside of our party. An golden opportunity missed!

Most GOP delegates are unaware that it is possible for delegates to introduce a motion to kick McCain or other RINOs out of the party. Or worse, they actually actively oppose the move, often for incoherent reasons.

It is critical for conservatives to understand that they hold the power in their own hands, as delegates, to eliminate corrupt politicians from inside the party. The Republican Party is a corporation, and it's "Board of Directors" is essentially the delegates and the Executive Committee they elect. The delegates have the right to do whatever they want with the party.

To showcase this point, with a simple majority vote the delegates at a convention could disband a major political party in their state. If you can destroy a party and basically kick everyone off the ballot with a simple majority vote, then it is obvious that one single politician can be kicked out of the party for violating it's principles.

In fact, parties have often removed politicians from their ballots for violating standards of ethical conduct, even when no illegal action has committed.

That is an arbitrary action, yet completely permissible under most state and party laws.

There may have been some who, while in favor of the initial rebuking censure of McCain, probably worried John McCain was too strong of a politician that he could of won as an independent, so they gave in to a distorted "political reality" and let him stay in the party to avoid fracture. But the point is still the same, should the party choose unity or principle?

The reality is, the establishment GOP are trying to trick us into destroying ourselves. Even if the party is unified, **no one will vote for it if it has no principles**. Principles win.

And for far too long, the GOP has tried to play the 51% game. This is a losing recipe for conservatives in a Republic. There is almost never a time in history where 51% of the public are right about *anything*. The founders understood the "fallen nature of man" and were adamantly against Majoritarianism, or rule by majority, which is why they created a Republic with strict minority rights.

If you ask someone today, who chooses our leaders, they will often suggest the voters and if asked the percentage needed to win they will reply 51%.

"Remember, success for a politician is 50% plus one." - Vice President Dick Cheney

Even that disturbing sound bite is inaccurate. Due to the electoral college system and gerrymandered Congressional districts, it is hard to say the real percentage required.

But the true reality is, less than 0.1% of the voters determine who will be President. And they don't do it at the ballot box. They do it at party conventions. For proof of this, we only need look back at the 1968 and 1972 Democratic conventions. Specifically when McGovern failed to take over the party in 1968, he didn't give up. Instead, he tried a new strategy: control the executive committees.

After his 1968 failure to get enough delegates for the Democratic nomination, McGovern took over a Committee in the party and introduced reforms that allowed his delegates to take over the party in 1972 for his radical agenda against the will of the vast majority of Democratic voters.

Afterwards they did lose the election because they were too radical and far-left, but they demonstrated a clear truth about the political system in America. A few thousand delegates control everything: they choose the Presidential nominee and set up the party rules.

Eventually they won complete control of the Democratic party. Delegates control everything. It is the GOP and Democrat party executives who ultimately put the names on the ballot for every partisan political office in the land. With a simple up or down vote at the party conventions, party platforms are changed, but there is a power deeper within the party...

The party itself can even re-select who is on the party ballot. It seems like the parties have forgotten they hold that power, or fear using it may "alienate" general election voters.

Sometimes they do it, especially on smaller fish. As recently as March of 2015, the Mississippi Democratic Party removed a state senate candidate from the ballot, because of arbitrary "residency" requirements that the party itself set forth.[i] Democratic Party officials were the judge and jury, not a court of law.

But a more clear example was during the 2014 elections, Alabama GOP kicked off a dozen and a half GOP candidates from the ballot because they were not true Republicans.[ii] Many had donated to democrats even!

One group, www.governmentalreform.org, is even heading up a nationwide plan to use this delegate process to control who our House, Senate, and Presidential candidates are.

In fact, they are the only conservative or libertarian group I can think of that is playing the "delegate game" and which understands that trying to win over 51% is almost impossible now for the GOP. It is harder and less rewarding to win a Presidential election than it would be to take over the Democratic Party.

It's rather unfortunate that very few people understand how much power a delegate has.

The few thousand delegates at the Republican and Democratic conventions select our Presidents each cycle. With no viable third party, those few thousand delegates effectively choose the leader who will govern our country and it's over 320 million American residents.

Proportionally speaking, even if you add the 2,380 Republican delegates with the 4,047 Democratic delegates you come to a total of 6,427 delegates. Those delegates have a power that is at least equal to the 125 million voters who vote in a Presidential general election.

If their power is equal, that means a single delegate carries the power of 20,000 voters. Conservatives could easily do more good by being an activist delegate introducing motions to censure corrupt politicians, than they would do by voting their whole lives.

And their power is not equal!

Those six thousand four hundred people decide who will rule America. Because there is no viable third party system, the **general election voters only get to decide between the candidates that <u>delegates have chosen</u>**.

And if you live in an early primary state like Iowa, New Hampshire, South Carolina, or Florida, then your power as a delegate is multiplied further.

So it is important for conservatives, libertarians, and populists to unite and coordinate their efforts against establishment politicians. Join governmentalreform.org and any other group that fights the crucial delegate battle. More importantly, join your local Tea Party and convince them to become delegates.

Despite supposedly being activists, it is appalling that less than 1 in 10 tea party members become the all-important Precinct Chairmen or delegates to their local county, district, or state conventions!

Ted and Rand: Leaders Emerge

Imagine a GOP today without Ted Cruz or Rand Paul. It's a GOP that would be dying or dead. These two political "superstars" have breathed life back into the party.

The simple fact is, the uninspiring John McCain and the stiff moderate Romney lost in a resounding defeat for elitists and "moderates" who think compromising on your values to win elections and "maintain unity" is the path to go.

Had these two "extreme" firebrands not shown up, those establishment politicians who think "selling out" is the way to win, may not have even had a party to return to. Many conservative pundits like Rush Limbaugh had started toying with the idea of disbanding the Republican party altogether.

It was the appearance of new and popular leaders like Ted Cruz, Rand Paul, Mike Lee, and others after 2010 that kept the party alive.

Rather than being grateful their party is still alive and recognizing the upstanding individuals who were reviving it from it's almost-dead state, the establishment GOP politicians have actually taken to attacking the very newcomers they owe their livelihoods to.

It truly is "biting the hand that feeds you" for the party establishment which would no longer exist, to attack the source of their own redemption.

Make no mistake, the party truly was on the brink. Many politicians and pundits don't realize the dire straits the GOP was in after the disastrous 2008 elections and while Romney tried his best to run a "positive" and stiff "traditional" campaign, not even a slick rhetorical master like him could bring it back because his ideas were old and boring.

Romney (or McCain for that matter) never excited the base. Compare that with Obama!

Obama had rejuvenated the Democratic party by ignoring the "moderates" and instead employing rhetoric that inspired his base. It didn't matter that in the end, that Obama didn't deliver anything his own base wanted. What mattered to his base was that they felt "heard". And Obama, who had been a "community organizer" before going into politics, knew exactly how to rile up communities but also how to engage their leaders and make them feel "heard" and hopeful.

The same methods don't work on most of the GOP: we want results. If a candidate makes the claim that they will be a conservative President as McCain and Romney did in their elections (albeit halfheartedly) but they don't have the track record to make such a claim, the base of the GOP will not be excited.

At best, the GOP was holding their nose. Many GOP voters called their nominee the "lesser of two evils", giving up on having a principled candidate in favor of a "winner".

But then, the "unthinkable" happened: the candidates that the establishment strategists like Karl Rove and deceptive pollsters like Frank Luntz said would "win" in a landslide, instead lost by large margins.

So we'd given up having a principled candidate in favor of a moderate candidate who could "win", but even then, they lost! It's like they only had one task, winning, and couldn't even do that! At that point what use was the GOP anymore?

Many pundits, like Rush Limbaugh were already starting to toy with the idea of "disbanding" the GOP and entering the Democratic Party (not a bad idea at all).

The idea seemed like our last option: if we "can't beat 'em, join 'em" and then try to change them from within. But the plan carried many risks of potential failure. Such talk of ending the party suddenly stopped because a new political movement was born: the Tea Party!

What any new movement needs are heroes. Champions who will fight for the cause and lead it's people to victory. Initially, those leaders came from a mixture of places whether on TV led by Rick Santelli who called for a "tea party" to protest Obama's bailouts, or in politics by the new politicians in 2010 like Rand Paul or Mike Lee.

Ted Cruz was a little later to the party, arriving in 2012 after defeating the establishment's handpicked choice of David Dewhurst who had millions of dollars from special interests backing him.

These leaders not only excite the "base" of the party, they <u>are the base</u>. Rand Paul had been the founder of the Kentucky Taxpayers United group that tried to fight local state government tax increases. He'd had experience helping out on his father's campaigns, but mostly contented himself to his private sector work as a doctor.

Ted Cruz also had never ran for political office before. He had been in government, but only as an appointed official. He was the first Hispanic to serve appointed as a clerk to a Chief Justice of the Supreme Court. Later in life, Cruz was appointed Solicitor General by then-Attorney General Greg Abbott. A close friend of Cruz, Greg Abbott became Governor of Texas in 2015 running as an adamant Tea Party supporter.

Ted Cruz had never run for office, and had even gone back to the private sector for years after his job as Solicitor General. But when the Tea Party rose up, Ted Cruz felt inspired to get involved.

Both of these men were civilians who, while they had been active in trying to get government to "behave better", had not become politicians. It wasn't until economic crisis and ensuing Tea Party rebellion that they rose when their country needed them. And yet, there may be more that unites them than meets the eye...

Freedom Lives in Texas

Besides their love of freedom, there is a common thread between Ted Cruz and Rand Paul. It's something fundamentally important but almost never mentioned: both Senator Cruz and Senator Rand Paul were raised in Texas.

But it's not just those two: a full five of the Presidential candidates were raised in Texas. But I believe the state had an especially strong impact on the lives of Ted Cruz and Rand Paul.

Yet simply stating that they are Texans does no justice to the extraordinary implications of just what it means to be Texan. Or to how having lived in Texas changed them, their families, and their perspectives. In order to truly understand the biographies of these two Senators, a little background on what it means to be Texan is required.

There is a sort of love of freedom and rebellious nature that unites Texans, after all...

As a Texan myself, I will be delighted to guide you through some highlights of a famous Texan whose brashness closely resembles that of Ted Cruz and whose cunning Texan stratagems are reminiscent of Rand Paul's political skill and strategic vision. This man is a man who I believe embodies the spirit of the Republic of Texas: Sam Houston.

Most Americans are aware, especially in light of the recent History Channel miniseries "Texas Rising", that Sam Houston was the Texan who led the Revolution for Texas Independence. Many are also aware that he was the Governor of Texas and refused to allow it to join the Confederacy and was removed from power by pro-Confederate forces. But few know the full story of this incredible man.

Sam Houston holds the honor of being the <u>only man in American history</u>, perhaps in World History, ever voted to be governor of <u>two different states</u>: Sam Houston was the governor of both Tennessee and Texas.

What led Houston to Texas is a little known event: Houston had been in D.C. trying to expose the U.S. government frauds against the Cherokee Native Americans when a Congressman who profited from that fraud, Ohio Congressman William Stanbery, made slanderous accusations against Houston.

Houston beat the Congressman with a hickory cane, and Stanbery fired a pistol back at Houston: luckily for Houston, it misfired and he survived. Congress, not a judge, ordered Houston's arrest, one of the few times Congress has ever done so.

The famous Francis Scott Key who wrote the U.S. anthem, "Star Spangled Banner", agreed to be Sam Houston's defense lawyer. Despite the famous lawyer's help, Houston was found guilty, and fined $500 which was a lot of money for the time. Rather than pay the large sum of money, which was a sort of political punishment levied by his political opponents, Sam Houston fled to Mexican controlled Texas.

The rest of Sam Houston's history is better covered by a large variety of movies. While much focus has been on the Alamo, more recently Sam Houston's life has been a subject of great interest.

Like Texas itself, Sam Houston is a bundle of contradictions. A man of can-do attitude, independent spirit, who achieved great things but was known to get drunk on more than one occasion. He worked hard and played hard.

But Sam Houston's bold and brash independent nature, like most Texan's, should not be mistakenly lumped together with irrationality or foolishness. Instead it's more of the contrarian nature of Texas, which we will get to later when discussing Rand Paul and his contrarian father.

While eager to declare independence from Mexico despite being outnumbered more than 20 to 1 in population, Sam and Texas were not eager to rush to a defeat. But when cornered...

Texans fight like no other. At the Alamo, a few hundred men held out against thousands of Mexican soldiers who threatened them with no quarter. Later at Goliad, Mexico massacred 400 unarmed Texan prisoners.

Texas may have started the war by declaring Independence, but Mexico was winning it. Yet the fearless nature of Texans made them eager for revenge, and highly opposed to retreating.

Despite calls to avenge them quickly, Sam Houston managed to convince his men to calmly retreat in a long march that would of demoralized most armies. Not Texans. We bided our time, and then struck.

Outnumbered, Houston waited for the right moment and found it on April 21, now known as "San Jacinto Day": he won a 25-to-1 victory and captured the President of Mexico.

As a relevant sidenote: the Texas Nationalist Movement, a group calling for independence from the United States, successfully passed a new law in May of 2015, allowing Texans to purchase and use fireworks to celebrate each year for "San Jacinto Day" on April 21. Previously, it had been illegal. The bill also made it legal to do so on Texas Independence Day on March 2nd.

More importantly, that same Texas Nationalist Movement has been collecting signatures for independence: and is on target!

If they manage to reach 75,000 signatures, independence will be put on the ballot in Texas. The state government doesn't allow initiatives or referendums, but the TNM movement found a "loophole" in the GOP party rules allowing them to put Independence on the GOP's 2016 Primary ballot.

What would Sam Houston think? The man opposed Texas joining the Confederacy in 1861 so what would he think of Texas independence more than a hundred years later?

He'd be for it. A bundle of contradictions, we Texans are. It was the circumstances. Like many Texans, Sam Houston was extremely opposed to slavery. As Texas' US Senator, Sam Houston voted against slavery as early as 1848. While as Governor of Texas, Sam Houston opposed joining the CSA in 1861 because it was over "damnable" slavery, but Houston also said this in favor of independence:

"Texas will again lift its head and stand among the nations. It ought to do so, for no country upon the globe can compare with it in natural advantages."

- Sam Houston

Houston was a man of principles, which means looking at the circumstances of the time.

Sam Houston was opposed in 1865, because it was for the wrong reasons (slavery) and at the wrong time: Texas had a relatively small population and economy at the time, whereas today Texas is the 12th largest economy in the world, equal to a "Great Power" like Australia.

Sam Houston was brilliant yet troubled. Sam opposed the Confederacy, but he also refused to fight against his fellow Texans when Lincoln offered him an army to command. Rough and straight talking, but yet able to be diplomatic. Understanding geopolitics but not giving into pressure from either side, whether from your allies (like within the party) or the enemy. Always negotiating from strength.

It's Texans like him who are the perfect match for a Presidential candidate: someone who needs to be strong and fierce, but yet calm and diplomatic. That's the sort of man Texans are. Brash, bold, determined, and in some ways contrarian. It's the sort of man America needs.

America needs a person to smash down the barriers of Political Correctness in the same way Sam Houston spoke out against slavery in the South in 1861 even though it cost him his career: he was removed from both the Senate and Governor positions because of his stances against slavery. We need bold leaders like him, willing to take a stand against their own party as Sam Houston did.

But we also need it done in that polite, yet boldly contrarian way that Sam did it which can reach the hearts of the voters. The charm of the Texan folksy rhetoric doesn't hurt either!

Perhaps that's why so many of our current Presidential candidates are Texans. Nearly all of the candidates are trying to employ a brash, bold "straight-talking" type of behavior that is clearly attempting to emulate the popularity of the charming Texan way of talking and living. If you count Eisenhower (born here), Texas has produced more Presidents than any state west of the Mississippi!

Who is Rand Paul?

When anyone votes for a President, they should first know who they are voting for. Before we get to Ted Cruz, we will cover the life experiences of Rand Paul and his past.

Like Ted Cruz, Rand Paul is a Texan. Another similarity is that they were not born in Texas but are "transplant Texans" who moved shortly after birth and were raised here.

Which is no different from this author's own experience of moving to Texas in my early childhood and being raised here.

Rand was born in Pennsylvania, but his family moved to Texas in 1968, when he was only 5 years old, a roughly similar age to Cruz. He was raised in Lake Jackson, Texas which is located in Brazoria County named for the Brazos river, it was Washington-on-the-Brazos nearby where Texas declared it's independence.

Rand Paul's ties to the Texas GOP run deep. In 1976, Rand Paul's father was elected as GOP congressman. When Rand was only 13 years old, he went to the GOP National Convention, as his father led the Ronald Reagan GOP delegates from Texas.

The Chairman of the Texas GOP, Steve Munistieri, views the native son as one of the leading frontrunners and said that Rand Paul is, "...objectively one of the three most likely people to get the nomination."[iii]

Paul grew up heavily influenced by the libertarian views of his Texan father. But some might say he might have been frustrated by the lack of progress his father made. He likely saw that Ron could have gotten further up the ladder by refining his talking points and that certainly shapes Rand Paul's worldview.

He went to Brazoswood High School in Texas, played football, and then went to many universities, but first to one in Texas.

Rand's first university was Baylor University in Waco, Texas. It was founded by Protestant Baptists in 1844, and it's first major donation was given by Sam Houston who was the "founding father" of Texas.

The university is imbued with that Texan independent spirit, but tempered by it's Baptist religious views much like it's founding donor, Sam Houston himself. When there, Rand Paul would join the local Young Conservatives of Texas as well as the "Noze Brotherhood", a fraternity of jokesters that would play pranks.

Paul, ever the ambitious young fellow, tried to find a way to skip past the 4 long years of university and move more quickly into serious study and closer towards a paying job. At the time, Medical Universities didn't "technically" require a 4 year degree. So Rand applied to his father's alma mater, Duke University. What's more surprising, is that Rand got in! So Rand Paul has the distinction of being one of the few medical doctors to skip getting a 4 year degree.

Now, whether this was due to his Congressman father's connections, status as the son of alumni, or his promising potential and good grades, is unsure. He finished his medical doctorate at the young age of 25, compare that to today's average graduation age of 33!

This young, skip the bureaucratic nonsense, "get to brass tacks" mindset is almost stereotypically Texan. The Texan author writing this book also had skipped high school and went to University at age 15.

In fact, the very phrase itself "get down to brass tacks" comes from Texas, and Rand shows he is serious about getting to the good parts of life, government, and politics, without putting up with the insufferable, bureaucratic nature of the game.

By all accounts Rand Paul is a bona-fide "naturalized" Texan, but unlike Ted Cruz who stayed in Texas, Rand was led away from his native lands, by a Yellow Rose!

When he studied surgery he met a woman from Kentucky, Kelley Ashby. He fell in love and they got married while he was studying. When deciding where to start his medical practice and start a family, they decided to move to Kelley's home state of Kentucky.

Showing his charitable nature and perhaps trying to prove the point of the Libertarian views he inherited, Rand started a non-profit in 1995 to provide free eye care, called Southern Kentucky Lions Eye Clinic. Juggling work with charity was not too much for him, and Rand even got involved in politics by founding the influential Kentucky Taxpayers United which fought the Kentucky state legislature's taxing and spending for years.

But eventually the group disbanded and Rand Paul had contented himself to private life. That was, until the Tea Party awoke the nation. Rand answered the call in 2010 and from there has grown into a national figure with a large and loyal following.

Who is Ted Cruz?

As we laid out in the previous chapter, Ted Cruz is a Texan. Not by birth, but a "naturalized Texan". In a way, his family already had roots in Texas before his birth. Both of his parents were involved in the oil business. His father Raphael Cruz attended the University of Texas. His mother studied math at Rice University in Houston, Texas.

The young Ted Cruz grew up in Texas, attending Faith West Academy in Katy, Texas. More impressively, he was the Valedictorian of Second Baptist High School in Houston.

It was at this time in Houston, not very far from Rand Paul in fact, that Ted Cruz came into contact with the libertarian "heroes" of the free market. Thinkers like Friedrich Hayek. Ted Cruz resided in Texas not very far from Ron Paul's congressional district in fact. He even studied Ludwig von Mises, the economic thinker that the Paul family most respects.

In a way, Rand Paul and Ted Cruz grew up close in location but also close in ideology. They even both pursued doctorates. While Rand Paul's was in medicine as explained previously, Ted Cruz chose a different path. Ted Cruz was fascinated by the rule of law in the United States.

This fascination was deep seated in the Cruz family after Raphael Cruz fled the brutal dictatorships in Cuba. He fled Batista's tyrannical regime and bemoaned Cuba falling into the hands of Castro who turned it into his property, a personal plaything for the dictator.

In pursuing law he first went to Princeton. While there, Ted Cruz was #1 in debating almost all the time. Ted Cruz in 1992 won the first place for both the United States and first place in the international North American Debating Championship. Cruz went to Harvard Law School but keep debating this time as a member of the Harvard team, almost winning but losing to Australia semi-finals in 1995.

Clearly, Ted Cruz was an up-and-coming professional. Cruz was known for being articulate, intelligent, and industrious. Not only did he graduate *cum laude* from Princeton but Ted Cruz actually graduate ***magna cum laude from Harvard Law School.***

That is probably one of the greatest achievements academically that anyone can make, yet Ted Cruz almost never boasts of this! Other candidate brag about their barely passing graduation of lesser universities, but Ted Cruz humbly leaves his graduating in the top 10% of Harvard Law School out of his rhetoric.

Personally, I think Ted Cruz needs to emphasize this more! Even most of his own supporters are unaware because Cruz makes no point of mentioning it. Maybe Cruz is concerned the mention of "Harvard" or "Princeton" might turn off his base who are opposed to establishment candidates.

I think Ted Cruz needs to own it!

Recognizing such impressive achievements, it is then no wonder that Ted Cruz become the first Hispanic clerk to a Supreme Court Chief Justice after graduation. Serving the Reagan appointee William Rehnquist, the last truly conservative Chief Justice, Ted Cruz would spend years analyzing the complex legal issues America faced.

Rehnquist's influence was also strong on Ted Cruz. The Chief Justice and friend of Ronald Reagan, was a big advocate of 10th amendment "state's rights", and was the first Justice to actually strike down Congressional law for exceeding the Commerce Clause which had never been done since the 1930's.

That type of strong Conservatism was imbued into Ted Cruz. After serving as clerk, Cruz went into private practice. But he did not serve random "corporate interests" like many lawyers. Cruz worked to defend conservatives, like the National Rifle Association and worked on the testimony to impeach Bill Clinton.

Ted Cruz was then hired to work in the Justice Department as an associate deputy attorney general. He was promoted to work as the Director of Policy Planning at the U.S. Federal Trade Commission and got to see first hand how bureaucracy stifles business. He set out to try and simplify the FTC and help promote business growth.

Ted was noticed with all of the good work that he did. In 2003 he was appointed by the Attorney General of Texas, Greg Abbott, to be his Solicitor General.

That same Greg Abbott would later go on to become the current Governor of Texas who swept away Rick Perry (who resigned to "run for President" but really knew Abbott was going to take him down) during a storm of Tea Party support.

Greg Abbott appointed Ted Cruz to take a "leadership role in the United States in articulating a vision of strict construction."

Taking the lead as Solicitor General is something Ted Cruz did, indeed! Ted Cruz currently holds the record in Texas, and among Congress, for having argued the most before the Supreme Court.

In a total of nine separate cases, Ted Cruz fought for conservatism. There was only one flaw in his otherwise impeccable career: for some reason, the Attorney General's office refused to fight Lawrence v. Texas. It's unknown who made the call, whether Greg Abbott, Cruz, or Rick Perry. To be fair, the Court was hopelessly stacked against Texas.

On the plus side, one of his greatest victories was convincing the Supreme Court that the "International Court of Justice" rulings were not binding in domestic law, effectively neutering the globalists attempt to force "international law" onto the US against it's will.

For his outstanding work, Ted Cruz is consistently viewed as a conservative fighter.

Not only that, but Ted Cruz has been viewed as a historically great lawyer. Ted Cruz was rated one of the top 25 Texan lawyers of all time by "Texas Lawyers" and in the top 50 "Best Litigators under 45" in the entire nation by "American Lawyers", the nationwide version.

Ted Cruz even won the Best Brief Award by the National Association of Attorneys General, a group consisting of all 50 of Attorney Generals of all 50 states, for his U.S. Supreme Court briefs in 2003, 2004, 2005, 2006, and 2007. Needless to say, being viewed as the best by all 49 of your other peers for many years in a row is quite an achievement!

It's the equivalent of winning "Best Actor" at the Oscars, but for 5 years in a row!

After this amazing stint as solicitor general, however, Ted did not pursue a political career. He certainly could have, if he wanted to. Instead, Ted went back to the private sector.

Is Ted Cruz Eligible?

Now that we know how great Cruz has been for conservatives, we must address a thorny issue. In the previous pages of this book, we mentioned that Ted Cruz was not born in Texas but certainly raised here and is definitely a "naturalized" Texan.

But where was he born? Canada. Some readers, if unaware, might be shocked to hear this. Maybe they are thinking this makes Ted Cruz ineligible to be President.

I can assure you, Ted Cruz is eligible.

However this is a slightly complex issue. This requires an in-depth understanding of what it takes to be a "natural-born citizen". There are actually basically three kind of "factions" that all disagree on "natural-born" citizenship.

But to summarize, each of these factions has a "school of thought" on natural-born status.

School of Thought #1: The Public

The public for the most part, believes the term "natural-born citizen" implies that you have to be "born on American soil" to be President. Most Americans believe this.

The entire "birther" scandal for the most part revolved around this misconception that American soil is what determines eligibility for the Presidency. It stems from an oversight....

The law that people gain citizenship by the location of their birth is called "jus solis", literally "right of soil". During the time of the Founders, almost no countries used this policy. When the Founders wrote the Constitution, America, Britain, and most of the world used "jus sanguis", literally "right of blood".

What this meant was that citizenship was conferred not by the location of the birth, but by to whom the child was born. Parentage was the sole determining factor for natural citizenship.

The confusion stems from the 14th Amendment. Originally designed to give all slaves citizenship, it somehow was twisted against the intent of the writer into conferring citizenship on all those born on American soil even into the future, when it was originally supposed to be a one-time event.

It was basically to solve the "stateless" status of former slaves. They were technically foreigners "immigrated" to America who were never given citizenship. The words of the 14th Amendment state, "subject to the jurisdiction thereof" which is why anchor babies are not citizens because they were illegal and not subject to our jurisdiction.

So with that confusion out of the way, we can now understand that parentage is the only true source of "natural-born" citizenship...

But the confusion doesn't stop there. There are two more schools of thought relating to parentage.

School of Thought #2: The Politicians

When John McCain announced he was running for President, the public had a clear problem with it: the U.S. had a presence near the Panama Canal, and John McCain's military father was stationed there. During that time John McCain was born on "foreign" Panamanian soil.

The Congress quickly cleared up any confusion and declared McCain had the right to be President because of his parentage. They had, correctly, taken the position of the founders: that parentage determines if a candidate is "natural-born".

Later, however, we come to the question of just what kind of "parentage". Which has to be American? Both? One? Which ones?

When Barack Obama ran, his mother was clearly a U.S. citizen. So why was there any "birther" scandal at all?

Why didn't Obama just point to his mother and end the debate right there?

There are some who say it is because Obama must have applied as a "foreign student" to get scholarship aid to Harvard, which would be a felony crime, and that is why he gave up his law license and spent millions to seal his Harvard records.

But it may be that the government is afraid the truth about "natural-born citizenship" will come out. And this is where the currently accepted Federal Government positions comes into conflict with the final school of thought.

The politicians have decided that "one" parent of either gender is sufficient for one to have "natural-born" status. There are some who say there is clear proof, straight from the founders, that this is incorrect.

School of Thought #3: The Strict Interpreters

Upon a proper examination of the Constitution, it's intent, and the meaning of the words of the time, it is clear that "natural-born" citizenship was intended to be of a person descended from an American citizen in the paternal line. That is to say, born of an American citizen father.

What is surprising is that the birthers never took this position on Obama who had a Kenyan father. Instead, they argued about his irrelevant birthplace. The fact Obama's father was not an American citizen was not disputed. It would of been an easy victory. The problem was, public opinion would view this as extremely sexist to say "natural-born citizenship" comes only from fathers.

But in the "Law of Nations", the rulebook used by the Founding Fathers to write the Constitution, the term "natural-born" refers to birth by a father citizen of the country.

This is where we get into the same argument as that of the "Original Intent" vs. the "Textualism" of some on the Supreme Court: should the Constituton be interpreted by using the intent of the framers? Or should we interpret only the literal text?

There are currently many laws against discriminating against women, but as the term "natural-born citizen" in the Constitution was written with a "sexist intent" of only granting it through the male-line, advocates of a Strict Constructionist interpretation would say that to change it's "intent" requires a constitutional amendment. Like many idealists, these people hope for respect of the "intent of the Founders" rather than skirt it on technicalities.

Whether or not we like it, the election of Obama has set a clear precedent. The government itself has stated Ted Cruz is eligible. No Presidential candidate has filed suit against him. Ted Cruz is eligible. Within the Textualist approach, Ted Cruz is natural-born.

Rhetoric Makes All the Difference

What is shockingly profound about these two men, Rand Paul and Ted Cruz, is not the differences between them, but how those differences are perceived by those around them.

While Rand Paul is invited onto liberal talk shows like the Bill Maher show, where the far-left progressive actually said, "I'm not sure who I'm going to vote for next time", the borderline Communist even said he might vote for Rand and called him the "most interesting politician".

Rand Paul is also invited frequently onto the Daily Show with John Stewart, a progressive outlet that openly mocks more socially conservative candidates. When on the show, John Stewart treats Rand with a deference and respect he would not show to a normal GOP candidate.

One might be tempted to think there is a conspiracy if compared with Ted's treatment...

47

While Paul gets praises, his counterpart Ted Cruz is conversely unanimously decried by the media. Donny Deutsch called Ted Cruz "scary", "dangerous", and "slimy". He is regularly bashed and insulted even by the same people (Maher, John Stewart, etc.) that Rand Paul was adored by.

When Rand Paul did his famous filibuster for 13 hours, even liberal talk show hosts praised him for it. When Ted Cruz stood up to filibuster for an astounding 21 hours, he was derided, ridiculed, and mocked by the same media that lavished praise on Paul's filibuster.

Why? The Rhetoric Game. Both of them play it, but they are targeting completely different audiences. Ted Cruz focuses his rhetoric on capturing the same Tea Party sentiment that made him a political star in the first place. In a way, Rand has capitulated verbally to progressive social values, which means he is not a threat to them. Ted Cruz, on the other hand, challenges their moral authority.

Rand Paul is focused completely on winning over moderates, minorities, young people and even many of the far-left liberals. That's why his rhetoric is aimed at a very different audience and while their policies at first glance might seem similar, their rhetoric is miles apart and has an shockingly different effect on how they are treated in the press.

Take the filibusters themselves for example. Rand Paul's filibuster was concise, well-timed, and picked an issue that a majority of all kinds of Americans, whether liberal, moderate, or conservative, agreed upon: namely that the government should not be able to order a drone strike on US citizens.

For many Americans, this was a real concern, especially after Obama assassinated an American teenager overseas, without a trial, who had not committed any crimes except that of being born to a radical father, both of whom were assassinated without trial by drone strike.

Rand Paul had a real effect by filibustering: slowing down the nomination of CIA Director Brennan. Rand Paul also achieved his goal, when he received a letter from the administration admitting they did not have the constitutional authority to assassinate Americans without due process (even though Obama had already assassinated Americans without a trial or even a military tribunal convicting them of treason).

By getting that admission, Rand looked victorious and he framed the matter as a victory for civil rights and a non-partisan issue.

Ted Cruz's filibuster target on the other hand was extremely partisan in nature: the Affordable Care Act, also known as Obamacare. Ted Cruz was rallying conservatives within the Republican Party to try to repeal the unpopular legislation. It was a move that could of worked if the GOP stuck together, but the moderates caved in.

Ted Cruz's filibuster, was argued to have no effect in the technical procedures of Congress and the same media that praised Rand Paul's drone strike and claimed it was "effective" then tried to portray Ted Cruz's filibuster as a pointless effort that did not succeed.

But at what point are we as a party? Are we only seeking to win at any cost? Do we have principles? Or do we give in on "controversial" issues and simply roll over for the Democrats until we can find the right issue at the right time to strike on?

The gay marriage debate is a perfect example. Social conservatives were drawing the line and each time liberals cross it, they draw a new one. First it was decriminalized, then civil unions, then the next line was gay marriage. And once that was made the law of the land, immediately the politicians had a new line to draw: religious liberty, basically the last ditch before the secularists forcibly convert you or throw you in prison for "hate speech".

Ted Cruz was only among three conservative Presidential candidates to show any outrage (the others: Carson and Huckabee). But even he then shifted his rhetoric to match that of his home state governor and attorney general who (paraphrasing) basically said "we lost, we give up, but here's a new line: religious liberty. Now don't cross that one!"

Rather than draw a line in the sand like the Alamo defenders and not cross it, they are showing cowardice by "re-drawing" the line every time it is crossed! **Now they are drawing it back to the very last line: religious liberty itself**, in order to be able to frame the debate in a way that libertarians like Rand Paul can come out and be for "religious liberty".

But what they don't realize is the media is in control of all debate framing. They will simply rephrase the issue. They already have begun to do so...

There are people who object to doing things against their belief like performing abortions or being forced to bake a cake for a gay couple. The left is already framing those people as "religious bigots".

It may not be working now....

But give it a couple of years, and the media will have pushed their "Overton Window", the range of acceptable thought that the P.C. Police allow, further and further to the radical, socialist, atheist "utopia" they desire.

Not very long ago, Hillary Clinton was standing behind her husband Bill Clinton who was signing the "Defense of Marriage Act" to ensure gay marriage is never legal nationwide. My how things have changed! Never before in history has the moral decline of a nation been so quick. Even the Roman Republic that America was modeled upon, took decades to fall to moral corruption and then finally to illegal immigration (Germanic barbarians).

Back when Bill signed the D.O.M.A., no one could imagine a mere few years later those same Democrats would now be praising a Supreme Court which forced gay marriage onto every state lawlessly and which Bill and Hillary encouraged to lawlessly ignore the very same Defense of Marriage Act they had signed and even championed in some ways.

Even less long ago, Barack Obama himself campaigned for President on an anti-gay marriage platform and Joe Biden bragged he came from a "slave state" with Confederate flags on many pick-up trucks. Today that same flag is on the verge of being outlawed speech.

Clearly, rhetoric can make all the difference. Personally, I favor a more direct, brash approach. But some people prefer a more conciliatory method but which might viewed by hardliners like myself as "appeasing" an enemy.

So the rhetoric of Cruz and Paul is an important difference, but there are others...

Main Differences

- Ted Cruz is more "conservative".
- Rand Paul is more "libertarian".

- Ted Cruz is the son of an immigrant.
- Rand Paul's family had deep roots.

- Ted's father: Pastor who fled dictatorship
- Rand's father: Libertarian political leader

- Ted Cruz absolutely opposes amnesty.
- Rand Paul favors amnesty.[1]

- Ted Cruz fights the media.
- Rand Paul tries to win them over.

- Ted Cruz is a brazen tactician.
- Rand Paul is an articulate strategist.

- Cruz is focused on immediate victory.

[1] "the 11 million, I think, are never going home, don't need to be sent home, and I would incorporate them into our society by giving them work visas and making them taxpayers"

- Rand is establishing a new ideology.

- Cruz filibustered Obamacare.
- Rand filibustered Drone strikes.

- Cruz team is aiming for a 10% flat tax.
- Rand Paul has a 14.5% "flat tax" plan.

- Cruz is willing to call out China and other "bad actors" on unfair trade.
- Rand Paul wants to eliminate tariffs, which would reward China and others.

- Cruz Issues: Obamacare/Immigration.
- Rand Issues: NSA/Civil Rights issues.

- Cruz: led fight to defund Obamacare.
- Rand: agreed to GOP "delaying tactics".

- Cruz is uncompromising.
- Rand calls self, "open to compromise".

That Time Ted Attacked Rand

One of the biggest differences between the two men is how they deal with their own party.

Ted Cruz fights with the GOP leadership, calling McConnell a "liar" who has betrayed the voters on the TPP. Cruz attacked Rand Paul over his coziness with GOP Senate Majority Leader Mitch McConnell, accusing Rand of saying one thing in public but then in private of siding with McConnell against Ted's effort to defund Obamacare and other issues.

It has been one of the only times the two Senators have ever been at odds. It is worth noting that Ted Cruz did not single out Rand Paul by name when making the accusations, but that it was more than clear who he was talking about. It was the first shot fired between them.

Where Rand Paul was set to compromise, Ted Cruz the GOP should keep it's promise to de-fund Obamacare no matter the political cost.

For some background on this fight, Rand and Mitch McConnell are the two Senators from Kentucky. Mitch McConnell is the powerful Senate Majority Leader who controls the bills that pass the GOP-controlled Senate.

Originally, McConnell was a Paul enemy. When Paul ran for Senate in 2010, McConnell endorsed his opponent and helped him raise money to beat Paul.

Yet after the election, rather than "fight the power" or hold a grudge, Rand Paul quickly befriended Mitch McConnell. It was very beneficial for Paul: McConnell helped Rand learn the ropes and gain committee chairs.

Even more recently, it has paid dividends: McConnell most certainly helped change Kentucky GOP rules to allow Rand to keep his Senate seat when he runs for President. Normally, a Senator would have to give up his seat to run for President.

Many in Kentucky criticized this move, saying Rand was treating the Kentucky Senate seat like a "back-up plan" rather than being fully devoted to the interests of Kentucky.

It reflects what was earlier outlined in the "differences" section: Ted Cruz is an uncompromising fighter who tries to win an immediate victory (like defunding Obamacare now) whereas Rand Paul is a pragmatist focused on a more long term strategy who is willing to "play the game" in order to climb up the political ladder.

The irony here is Rand Paul's base is actually more anti-establishment than even Ted Cruz's, so understanding this takes explaining...

Many Rand Paul supporters and perhaps Rand Paul himself, grew frustrated with the fact that his father, Ron Paul, never gained traction within the GOP.

Rand Paul views himself as the "bridge" between libertarians and conservatives, and is attempting to unite the two causes against a common enemy: the Democratic Party.

This frustration with his father's failures, may explain Rand's willingness to do what his father would not: compromise.

But those same compromises put at risk the very thing that made the Paul family special: their connection to libertarianism. Even conventional Libertarians are notoriously purist, with attempts at "compromise" often viewed as "selling out" to the statists.

Many libertarians' extreme distrust of government is derived from the idea or theory that a cabal of evil people rule the government. To them, compromise with evil is to do evil...

Rand Paul is in a difficult position: Libertarianism by itself cannot win the GOP nomination, but if Rand Paul continues down the path of compromise with the GOP establishment, he alienates the followers of the very ideology he champions.

When Rand instead tries to gain more support by appealing to Social Conservatives by abandoning libertarian positions on social issues, he also suffers losing the support of the more hardcore libertarians unwilling to compromise on their ideology.

For every social conservative supporter he gains, he loses at least one libertarian supporter. Rand had enjoyed a flurry of coverage after the 2012 elections when the liberal media gave him generous coverage. It was likely the media wanted to try and spin the 2012 election into a "defeat for social conservatism" and to push the "give up on social issues" narrative that many Libertarians advocate to the GOP, ignoring that Romney and McCain were social moderates.

It was the post-2012 election coverage that gave Rand Paul a much needed boost into a temporary status as the "Front-runner" at #1 in many polls. But it was only a temporary moment when many conservatives felt that "maybe" they needed to give in on social issues to be able to win elections.

But this sort of "give up our values in order to win" mindset risks <u>watering down both ideologies into the same defeatist establishment GOP type of candidates who have consistently lost the past elections</u> rather than going with the "time tested" strongly vocal social conservatism of winners like Reagan and Eisenhower.

Both John McCain and Mitt Romney were "moderates" on social issues, flip-flopping on many of them, using soft rhetoric, and both lost the election resoundingly among the socially conservative (but fiscally liberal) Hispanic and African American communities. It is only the aging and shrinking white demographic that is falling for socially liberal media propaganda.

It was, after all, the increased Black voter turnout that caused the Prop 8 voter ballot to ban Gay Marriage in California to succeed.

Conversely, Hispanics are overwhelmingly opposed to abortion. By not appealing to those communities' conservative values, by looking weak on the issues, by not attacking the other sides' vulnerabilities on social issues, Romney and McCain handed the election to the Democrats on a silver platter.

There is nothing more repulsive to those growing minority communities than a socially liberal fiscal conservative. In the end, due to the widespread poverty in these communities, they have prioritized the fiscal liberal policies of the Democratic party. They'd rather be fed by a corrupt government, than left to starve by a supposedly "moral" one.

Whether or not welfare actually helps these communities is irrelevant (it likely hurts them) because most of them think they need welfare.

In the end, it's a question of priorities.
Should we open our wallets and save our soul?
Or sacrifice our souls to save our wallets?

The question may solve itself: only a moral country will have the strength to resist the temptation to slide into socialism. You cannot resist fiscal liberalism without a strong social conservatism. If a people can't resist materialism, sexual vices, gluttony, or other temptations, it is highly unlikely they will not "vote themselves money" from the treasury.

An immoral people would have no desire to balance their budget. When a nation like ours becomes full of gluttons, drug addicts, sex addicts, porn addicts, alcoholics, or worse, they will have a strong desire to avoid work to pursue their hedonist desires. Even if they don't embrace socialism's promise money for nothing, they will be too addicted to their vices to get off their rears and protest or take action. Most of them, however, will gladly take the government's money.

*"**Democracy cannot exist as a permanent form of government. It can only exist until the voters discover that they can vote themselves money from the Public Treasury.** From that moment on, the majority always votes for the candidate promising the most benefits from the Public Treasury with the result that a **democracy always collapses over loose fiscal policy always followed by dictatorship.[i.e. Weimar Republic's Hitler]** The average age of the world's greatest civilizations has been two-hundred years. These nations have progressed throught this sequence: From bondage to spiritual faith; from spiritual faith to great courage; from courage to abundance; from abundance to complacency; from complacency to apathy; from apathy to dependence; from dependence back again into bondage."*

\- Alexander Fraser Tyler

Tyler inspired the Founding Fathers. Many of the founders have made similar quotes paraphrasing this one.

Their Tax Plans

Both Rand Paul and Ted Cruz have outlined either all or part of their tax plans. Rand Paul's tax plan is more "set in stone", while Ted Cruz is still formulating the entire specifics of his plan.

So first, let's start with Rand Paul and his plans for the IRS....

<u>Rand Paul Tax Plan</u>
The 14.5% "flat" income tax.

I have a number of objections right off the bat. Firstly, when you offer a huge tax deduction to the poor, I don't call it a "flat" tax. It's extremely progressive. Rand Paul leaves the poor with "no skin in the game", by offering a $50,000 tax deduction but no other deductions are allowed. This greatly simplifies the tax code, but means a majority of Americans would pay no income tax. This means the poor will happily call for more taxes since they pay none!

The plus side is Rand basically eliminates ALL other taxes: estate, payroll, gas tax.

But then he goes and does something that makes no sense: Rand Paul proposes to eliminate all tariffs.

This should be scrapped as it may backfire in an environment where workers are desperate for jobs and China is cheating on trade.

It's rather sad that Rand offers an uninspiring 14.5% income tax rate, and then eliminates tariffs. He has a missed opportunity: he could instead keep tariffs and offer a 10% rate by using tariff revenue to lower taxes.

Why should Americans pay higher taxes so that China can export goods more cheaply to the USA? Why should Americans pay MORE taxes so that foreign countries can flood America with their goods?

Why not have Americans produce instead?

But it's not too late for Rand. It's very early in the game, and Rand could simply state that he has heard the will of the voters and change his tax plan.

Yet the fundamentals here are still troubling. Rand Paul's $50,000 tax deduction is like handing the Democrats their progressive dream: the poor and middle classes will basically pay little to no taxes and almost all of the tax burden will be shifted to the upper 25% of Americans.

Rand Paul is also being slightly naive here by assuming that Democrats will leave the tax rate at an awkward 14.5% instead of raising it. With the poor and middle class opposition to tax rates out of the way, Rand's plan would virtually ensure taxes are raised to at least 20% if not 25% within a decade of it's enactment.

But again, I suspect Rand designed this plan mostly to win over voters and didn't quite think through the ideological implications.

Ted Cruz Tax Plan
10% flat income tax rate
Abolish the IRS

Ted Cruz's plan, on the other hand, makes no mention of tariffs thus far and is a plan in which supposedly everyone shares in the tax burden equally. The only deductions he has suggested would be for deductions for charity and mortgage interest. The Cruz campaign has not yet finalized their tax plans, however, and have said they are listening to voters and still crafting the ultimate proposal.

What Ted Cruz has said, so far is that it would be in the ballpark of 10% and that he'll eliminate some taxes (gas tax and capital gains tax are my recommendations).

But best of all, Ted Cruz wants to make taxation so simple it fits on a "postcard" that you simply mail in. Ted Cruz said he plans to abolish the IRS and instead have only a few dozen employees at Treasury take care of it.

Part of the reason it's important from an anti-tax perspective to not offer such a large exemption from taxes to most of the voters like in the Paul plan, is because then they have no "skin in the game".

To paraphrase, it's hard to be angry about taxes when you're not being taxed! This is why many yell for more taxes on the rich: they don't pay any taxes themselves!

So to summarize, Ted Cruz's plan may be harder to implement but is more likely to have "staying power" as it is low enough to please most, and structured so everyone has an interest in keeping taxes low.

Most importantly, unlike Rand's plan, Ted plans to abolish the IRS. Getting rid of the huge tax collecting machine will slow down any efforts to start raising taxes by potentially decades!

Best Tax Plan: NO TAXES!

Personally, I am sick of GOP politicians trying to squeak by with unimaginative, weak ideas on taxation. Ted Cruz and Rand Paul both offer good plans, better than their competitors so far, but they do not go far enough. At a time when the IRS was caught persecuting Tea Party groups, the nation is ripe for a bold plan to eliminate the IRS and get rid of the income tax.

Luckily, Ted Cruz offers to abolish the IRS but I worry that his plan to have Treasury take over aspects of it may lead to a situation where the Treasury Department morphs into a new IRS.

America needs get rid of the income tax altogether and we can do it in a way that doesn't reduce government revenue even! Taxing income creates a disincentive for companies and individuals to work harder and earn more money. It also harms America's global competitiveness.

Instead of taxation, America would be better served by a mixture of tariffs and issuing currency. What is surprising is that the anti-tax crowd is also anti-tariffs. The reality is, to truly be <u>against</u> taxes, you should be <u>for</u> tariffs.

For example, America could eliminate many taxes by levying a 10% tariff on nations which were manipulating their currency. like China, Japan, and the EU, which are doing it to steal American business.

Larger tariffs of 20% should be raised on enemy nations like Russia, Iran, and Belarus or on troublemakers like Mexico. Such tariffs would help deter such bad behavior, and also have the added effect of raising roughly $300 billion which is more than the gas tax and capital gains taxes combined.

By eliminating the gas tax, almost all products become cheaper because transportation costs are lowered and American drivers keep more cash which they can spend on the economy, further boosting it.

By eliminating the capital gains tax, the USA would encourage more investors, including foreign investors, to buy U.S. stocks, bonds, and other investments in the US market. This would be a tremendous economic boost.

And the "downside"? A tariff to replace that revenue, is actually a <u>benefit</u>: it encourages manufacturers to locate inside the USA. It is true that tariffs are a double edged sword which while raising revenue can also cause some harm, especially for a country that relies on exports. But the USA is a net "importer" country, which means we import far more goods than we export.

So that means the benefits far outweigh any potential negatives by an overwhelming ratio.

To those people who claim that enacting tariffs would mean a "trade war" they are grossly misinformed: even now, <u>many of the nations the USA has "free trade" with, those countries themselves tariff US-made goods</u>!

Yet the USA endures those tariffs, to keep those allies "favor". But such weakness from a superpower only encourages our allies to doubt us and enemies to mock us, while both profit by flooding our country with cheap, but poorly made goods. Sometimes even dangerous goods, like the lead-painted toys China sent our children which was poisoning them.

Besides, any loss in US exports would be more than made up for by gains taken from what is normally a US import. Maybe Japan would put more tariffs on US agriculture (which they already do despite our free trade agreements) and we might lose $2 billion in beef sales, but we would gain at least $50 billion in automotive sales because US car companies would become more competitive.

Clearly the benefits outweigh the risks!

Take Japan, who sends us over 1.5 **million** cars every year. The USA sends far less to Japan. What the USA does export, however, are things Japan cannot make themselves. Many US exports are patented pharmaceuticals, chemicals, military equipment, and things which Japan cannot produce for itself so it cannot reduce US exports by increasing tariffs.

So it is a win for us, with almost no negatives except maybe our President having to listen to the Japanese, Korean, and other Heads of State whining on the phone.

In addition, the USA also is the world's superpower with the greatest military on the face of planet. Most countries will not enact "retaliatory tariffs" against us because we could remove our military protection from them. The US military has bases all over the world, and our protection is very valuable.

For example, Japan and South Korea have large US bases and nearly 100,000 American soldiers are stationed there to protect them at our expense.

Yet these "allies" we are spending billions to protect both heavily tariff our goods unfairly and engage in currency manipulation. If we were to enact a tariff to punish their "cheating" on trade, and they want to threaten us back, we could simply withdraw our US troops, which would also further save us billions every year.

With Russian and Chinese aggression on the rise, now is the ultimate opportunity for America to start demanding countries either stop cheating on trade or accept a tariff. America cannot afford to both be the "police" of the world and suffer bad trade deals at the same time from those same "allies" we are spending so much to protect.

But again I would remind people most US exports are patented products or luxury goods cannot be made by the countries we would tariff. Their tariff would only serve as a tax on their own populace, rather than encourage local production. In our case, tariffs serve to replace taxes, and then to discourage imports and encourage US-based production. As a consumer nation, it is important we start to produce what we consume, or we will become overly reliant on foreign countries.

Let's use an example to illustrate how this works for both companies and workers in which the US places a tariff on nations that are unfriendly or cheating on trade and we eliminate the gas tax and capital gains tax by using that revenue.

Chevrolet and Ford would see their sales skyrocket as US-made cars become cheaper compared to Japanese and German cars. They hire thousands of workers, like "Detroit Joe". Joe has been unemployed for weeks, lives in U.S. government provided Section 8 housing, uses food stamps, and collects unemployment because he is a low skilled worker and can't find good-paying work because of bad trade policies and a flood of illegal immigrants.

When Ford re-opens a closed plant, he immediately rushes back for the job and gets it. He is given hope in life again, a good paying salary of $42,000 a year, and now the government saves nearly $10,000 a year because he is off of government welfare. He also gets health insurance which means US taxpayers will no longer have to foot his medical bills.

Then when "Detroit Joe" looks at his gas bill each month, he notices it is $30 lower because there is no gas tax anymore!

Then to further add to his joy, when he checks his investment account he notices most of his stock picks have gained more than he predicted. Why? Because foreign countries have rushed to invest in America when the capital gains tax was eliminated. This has led to boom in venture capitalism and company expansion. His sister "Detroit Jane", who was struggling with two-part time jobs like many Americans, finally got a good-paying job at one of these new companies and no longer asks him for financial help all the time.

Then as the cherry on top of all this, when "Detroit Joe" files his taxes, he is amazed to find that he doesn't have to pay any tax on his $6,000 in earnings in the stock market. This saves him roughly $900.

So he saves $360 a year from eliminating the gas tax, $900 a year from eliminating the capital gains tax. He now earns $32,000 more per year and saves $1,260 more per year than when he was on government welfare.

So he benefits a total of $33,260 and the US government saves $10,000 per year because he is no longer on welfare. There is also a benefit that all groceries, goods, and other products shipped by transportation would become about 2% cheaper because the elimination of the gas tax means transportation costs are lowered. This saves "Detroit Joe" another $150 a year.

So what is the down side?

"Detroit Joe" had to pay an extra $30 on a Sony Playstation and bought a US-made TV for $40 more than he normally would of because Samsung TVs are more expensive now and the US-made TVs are actually slightly cheaper now, whereas before they were more expensive.

If this didn't happen he would of bought a Korean "Samsung" TV. But the $40 he would of saved is outweighed by the $50 earned by an American TV maker who then hires more US citizens, perhaps a relative of "Detroit Joe" or of this reader! The effect multiplies itself.

But when Joe or others go to the grocery store or other stores, they notice they are saving about $400 a year because the elimination of the gas tax has dramatically lowered food costs.

This is the nature of tariffs. Sure maybe the average consumer might spend $50 a year more on foreign products because of tariffs, but if we use the revenue to eliminate the gas tax, we'd all save $300 or more per year which far out

The negative effect of the tariffs might be this: when he goes to the electronics store if he decides to buy a Sony TV it might cost him an extra $5.

Part of the reason tariffs have been unappealing in the past was because those offering the tariffs were usually Democrats who planned to waste the money on failed government programs.

But what is truly popular, is to eliminate taxes altogether by using tariffs on "bad actors".

When Mitt Romney helped lead a charge within the GOP to enact a tariff on China for cyber attacks and currency manipulation, and use the money to lower taxes, it was one of the few galvanizing moments of his campaign.

Unfortunately, Romney backed away like a coward and flipped his focus to less popular issues like entitlement reform. Had Romney stood his ground and been a champion of "workers" by helping bring back jobs from China, Russia, Mexico, Germany, and other countries that are cheating on their "free trade" agreements, he would of won in a landslide instead of losing!

Interestingly, during the writing of this book, Donald Trump entered the race and started advocating positions on trade that are giving voice to the concerns of many "economic nationalists" that want to fight back the economic subversion of China in trade. While Ted Cruz has embraced Trump's rise, Rand Paul is fighting it, tooth and nail....

Who is more likely to win?

Which brings us to the most important point of all. Who is going to win?

There are a number of scenarios that may unfold in the 2016 race for the Presidency. Both the Primaries and the General Election pose a number of great challenges for Cruz and Paul, as well as for the GOP in general.

Prior to the entry of Donald Trump recently as of the time of this writing, there was basically one main scenario that would play out in the GOP primaries.

The typical GOP scenario would run down in the usual way: about a dozen candidates run, eventually the moderates and establishment rally around one candidate to stop whichever conservative is gaining traction.

It was a two-way dynamic with the main fight between conservatives and moderates.

Usually, whoever can lead the pack of conservatives goes on to fight whoever is leading the moderate establishment and their elitist financial backers.

This all changed back in 2008 and 2012, a new dynamic was introduced: the libertarian "Ron Paul" wing of the party. Rather than just two candidates who duked it out, there was a three-way fight for the delegates that went on longer than usual.

This time, there may be a four-way brawl!

A new sort of group is coming onto the scene: the disaffected "Populists" who are sick and fed up of basically anyone who is a career politician. They hate stiff-necked talkers who read speeches off teleprompters and want a genuinely honest leader.

Basically there are no longer "wings" of the GOP anymore, but four major "factions" fighting for the nomination.

Faction #1: The Establishment

Jeb Bush
Chris Christie
Marco Rubio
Rick Perry
Carly Fiorina
John Kasich
Lindsey Graham

These are the guys who care about winning at all costs. They compromise all their values. They can't be trusted reliably on social issues or fiscal issues. Scott Walker and Fiorina would try to claim they are "Social Conservatives" but when push comes to shove, they "accept" Progressive Court decisions on social issues.

Faction #2: The Social Conservatives

Ben Carson
Mike Huckabee
Ted Cruz
Bobby Jindal

Faction #3: The Libertarians
Rand Paul
Ted Cruz

Really only two candidates even attempt to identify as Libertarians. Ted Cruz is a "libertarian-conservative" who leans more towards social conservatism than libertine style libertarianism. Rand Paul also attempts to maintain his own socially conservative positions against gay marriage and against abortion, usually staking a "state's rights" position. Problem is, the Supreme Court has forced a "one-size-fits-all" glove on the states. Rand is trying the "get government out of marriage altogether" tactic, but he may be forced to choose a side at some point.

Faction #4: The Populists

Donald Trump

A new faction is emerging in both parties of "Populists" which may shake up the contest.

Where they come down on the Populist movements may symbolize a key difference between Ted Cruz and Rand Paul.

While Ted Cruz is embracing Donald Trump's rise, encouraging his outspoken attacks against political correctness, Rand Paul is taking the opposite approach.

This is a fight that actually goes back 2,000 years. Back in the Roman Republic which the USA is modeled on, there were Populists. In fact, the word comes from "Populares", the name of the Roman faction which stood with the people against the "Optimates" in the Senate, the more Aristocratic side which favored the traditions of the "Founding Fathers" Romulus and Remus, respected Senate "decorum", and looked down on populist movements embracing the "vulgar" masses.

It is perhaps, then, no irony that Rand Paul's father, Ron Paul, was called the "Cicero" of our time by his fans. Now Rand picks up the baton.

It is clear that Donald Trump represents the Populares, the Populist side of the Republic, against the more tradition-favoring Aristocratic Optimates faction. While Rand Paul certainly is not an advocate of Aristocracy today, he is certainly the inheritor of the Optimate traditions and the most outspoken advocate of the Founding Fathers, who were themselves very similar to the slave-owning Aristocratic Optimates, particularly Brutus and Cicero.

Is Donald Trump a new Julius Caesar? Is Rand Paul the great new orator of Constitutionalism, the Cicero of our time, doomed to have his hands cut off and posted to the Senate doors as Cicero's were?

Where will Ted Cruz stand? Will he stand with the Populares, like Marc Anthony? Or will his affinity with the traditions of the Republic lead him, Trump's friend, like Julius' friend Brutus, to turn on him and rejoin the Optimates should Trump go astray?

Let's pray that more has changed since Rome's Republic 2,000 years ago than our attire! If only we could pass a law requiring Congressmen to wear togas! Maybe then, people might see that while our technology changes, human nature itself has not changed.

As was written in Ecclesiastes, "*What has been will be again, what has been done will be done again; there is nothing new under the sun.*"

There truly is nothing new under the sun!

In the end, Donald Trump might make a gaffe from which he can't recover. Perhaps America isn't repeating the same history as Rome but will attempt a restoration.

Maybe the Cicero wins election to Consul this time. Maybe Rand becomes President.

Or maybe someone in-between the two, like Ted Cruz, who is basically half-Optimate and half-Populares, will step in and unite the two feuding factions. Perhaps we will see the interests of both the traditions of our Republic and a respect for the Founders maintained while at the same time addressing the grievances of the vast majority of Americans suffering in this time of economic difficulty.

With the rise of the Populares, however, this election may be "Trump's to lose", and when this Julius Caesar stumbles, whoever is his loyal Marc Anthony that decries the (media) assassins, will be ready to swoop in and win the election. My bet, then, would be on Ted Cruz.

Conclusion

The two candidates Rand Paul and Ted Cruz both are dynamic, interesting Senators. In some ways, they are very similar: they both have large followings but are not mainstream candidates. They both prioritize fiscal issues over social issues, they both have Texan heritage, and they both carry a strong independent streak.

Both are allies of the tea party, both are fiscally conservative and desire a balanced budget. Both are leaders trying to get an amendment passed for a balanced budget and both are in favor of term limits.

But they also have many differences, especially in style. Ted Cruz is a firebrand that gets media headline and polarizes while firing up the conservative base to hold it's politicians accountable. When Cruz enters a liberal media outlet, the interview or debate usually ends with the media attacking Mr. Cruz or vice versa.

Rand Paul, harnesses his own firebrand father Ron Paul's Libertarian followers but tries to play the political game, wooing over Senate Majority Leader Mitch McConnell, reaching out to minority groups, going on the most liberal shows and being friendly to the progressive media, all in the hopes that doing so might allow him to take power.

Some of his diehard fans actually believe Rand is trying to be a small government Libertarian "Trojan Horse", hoping he can play the political game, win power, and not be corrupted by it. They hope he would use that power to shrink the government dramatically.

Yet that same game-playing has alienated many of his followers, who are calling him a "sell-out". It reminds me of a quote by the founder of Libertarianism, Murray Rothbard, who created Libertarianism but worried it could never become "mainstream" or if it did, it would destroy itself out of fear...

Murray Rothbard, Founder of American Libertarianism on when Libertarians win office:

*"here we face an inner problem and a paradox not only for libertarians, but for any radical, minority ideological movement. For **marginal movements attract marginal people**. Such movements are filled with what Germans call luftmenschen, people with no steady jobs, incomes, or visible means of support; **the sort of people who instinctively alienate the mainstream bourgeois Americans,** not so much by the content of their ideas, but by their style, lack of moorings, and "counterculture".*

*If a serious opportunity should arise… for the [Libertarian] movement to make a great leap into Middle America, into genuine influence in our society, **that Libertarian luftmenschen will react not with enthusiasm but in fear and trembling.** For far greater than their professed love of liberty is their hostility to bourgeois America."*

- Murray Rothbard

So in the political battle between these two, regardless of your personal preference, a betting man would put his bet on the Ted Cruz horse simply because it is hitched to a more reliable wagon: the social conservative bloc. Now there is even the new Trump factor to consider, and Cruz is poised to reap the benefit.

Part of the problem for Rand is his father's followers are often apathetic about voting. Many suggest that by **not voting** they "show their disapproval". Others say voting is "rigged" and pointless. They commit political suicide.

Libertarians themselves instinctively hate "politicians", which makes it hard to count on their vote. Libertarians view government power suspiciously, so it makes it a contradiction to run as a "libertarian politician" desiring power! A common question rings out from libertarians:

Why do you want power, if you claim you will not use it once elected?

It's essentially the point of the famed anarchist-monarchist J.R.R. Tolkien: only those who don't want the "Ring of Power" can be the ones to destroy it. Even then, it is very difficult.

Choosing leaders by popularity would be akin to if Frodo and the band of merry Hobbits decided to let people run for office to decide who will get the Ring of Power. Power-hungry Boromir would of won in a landslide, no doubt!

In such a situation, those who want to gain that power for themselves will work the hardest, night and day, to claw their way to power. They, like Boromir, see great power as a tool to be used, not something to be feared.

Whereas those best suited to carry the "burden of power" are the peaceful, happy, contented people like the Hobbits, who care not for politics and would mind their own business, tend their gardens, and enjoy a good smoke or drink like many middle class Americans.

This contradiction, that only those who don't want power are suited to wield it, is a part of the paradox of the human condition.

Many hold up Washington as an inspirational model of how the Republic should elect our Presidents, but the problem is, he was not truly a "President". He was a Warrior King.

Let me explain why....

The Presidential model of a Republic invites politicians to campaign for office. George Washington did not go around making speeches, and he even refused to campaign for office like Presidents do, he just relaxed in his home until he won the election in a landslide with no real political challenger to "debate" or media to give "interviews" to.

It can't really be called an "election" if the leader is "anointed" without a political challenger or it is considered vile to even run against him for office.

Washington was given power without trying. And why? Because of military victories. He was given power as a reward for leading the troops to victory. That is not a "President" but rather more akin to the great Warrior Kings of the past, like an Alexander the Great, Napoleon, or even a Julius Caesar.

George Washington was even offered the crown of America, but he had no reason to accept this. He was old and knew his death was at hand as most of his brothers had died. He also had no son. There was no direct heir to leave his kingdom. He died within two years of leaving office. His legacy became his heir.

The point is that power was bestowed on him as a reward for military victories, like a Warrior King. His legacy should not be viewed as proof that elections can produce people who are not power hungry, because he was not truly "elected" in the traditional sense. He did not campaign. He was rewarded with power for his great military service. He also fought in a crisis.

Only in a crisis that threatens our very survival would those who value family more than power, like Washington or a Baggins, be willing to sacrifice their peaceful lives in order to make a long and difficult journey/campaign.

Like the doom of Middle Earth, we now quite possibly face the end of America in our human and Earthly story, if our debt continues to grow and we face almost inevitable collapse.

Is a system that only produces good leaders when it is on the verge of collapse really such a good system?

Is it such a good system when good candidates only run because they fear for the survival of the country?

Is it a good political structure for libertarians if it almost never puts libertarians as the rulers?

Or which taxes us more than the British did?

At some point, the system is itself to blame!

Only during the fear of the cold war, did a Reagan emerge. Only during the fear of economic collapse, have the Paul and Cruz families decided to enter politics and suffer the scrutiny, attacks, and months-long difficulties of a political campaign.

And even then, we have to worry... during difficult times, Republics often elect charismatic dictators. Hitler was voted into power in a Weimar Republic created by the USA and closely modeled after our own American Republic. As was Robespierre.

Mao Zedong was even a congressmen in a Republic that was inspired by our American Constitution. It's founder Sun Yat Sen actually studied in the USA. The steps to dictatorship, whether Communist or Fascist, seems to almost always require a transition to a Republic along the way. There were free, elected Republics in both Russia and China before Communism.

Even Stalin's Republic, the Soviet Union, was deeply inspired by our American Republic and it's Union. It enshrined "freedom of the press" and "religious freedom" in their Constitution, like ours. It had courts and laws, constitutional protections, and more.

In a manner foreshadowing how America itself now lawlessly ignores the Constitution frequently, in the USSR, despite their USSR Constitution protecting "religious freedom" and granting many more freedoms than even the U.S. constitution does, like the "right to work" and "right to healthcare", it did not stop Stalin from terrorizing and murdering thousands of Orthodox Christians.

It isn't a piece of paper that protects anyone. The Soviet Constitution did not stop Stalin. Rather, America's Constitution is only effective so long as Americans treat it with a practically religious reverence. That reverence itself is the last line of defense and it is breaking apart.

But now there are many opponents of the Constitution, who openly "blaspheme" against it, like a heretical sect twisting it's meanings.

This heresy has now amazingly found it's way into the very heart of the U.S. government. The President issues illegal executive orders with no one challenging him. Congress passes unconstitutional laws on an almost daily basis.

Worse, the Supreme Court has even enacted laws that do not exist. Justice Scalia called it a "judicial putsch"[2] destroying the Constitution.

With the constitution no longer sacred, the elite try to reassure us with the oft-repeated lie that liberty is synonymous with Republics or Democracy. The truth is quite the opposite...

Or as Libertarian Mencken greatly stated:

[2] A putsch is defined by Merrian-Webster as "a secretly plotted and suddenly executed attempt to overthrow a government". Scalia said this because there was no amendment, not even a Congressional law, and no precedent for the gay marriage decision. Gay marriage advocates needed to follow the proper constitutional process and pass a gay marriage amendment, not illegally bypass the Constitution and force a newly invented law out of thin air on all the states.

*"**Liberty and democracy are eternal enemies**, and every one knows it who has ever given any sober reflection to the matter. A democratic state may profess to venerate the name, and even pass laws making it officially sacred, **but it simply cannot tolerate the thing**.*

In order to keep any coherence in the governmental process, to prevent the wildest anarchy in thought and act, the government must put limits upon the free play of opinion.

In part, it can reach that end by mere propaganda **[Political Correctness]**, *by the bald force of its authority; that is, by making certain doctrines officially infamous. But in part it must resort to force, i.e., to law.*

One of the main purposes of laws in a democratic society is to put burdens upon intelligence and reduce it to impotence.

Ostensibly, their aim is to penalize anti-social acts; actually their aim is to penalize heretical opinions. At least ninety-five Americans out of every 100 believe that this process is honest and even laudable; it is practically impossible to convince them that there is anything evil in it. In other words, they cannot grasp the concept of liberty.

Always they condition it with the doctrine that the state, i.e., the majority, has a sort of right of eminent domain in acts, and even in ideas; that it is perfectly free, whenever it is so disposed, to forbid a man to say what he honestly believes. **Whenever his notions show signs of becoming "dangerous,"[Racist, "Hate Speech", extremist, etc.]** *ie, of being heard and attended to, it exercises that prerogative. And the overwhelming majority of citizens believe in supporting it in the outrage.*

Including especially the Liberals, who pretend, and often quite honestly believe, that they are hot for liberty. They never really are.

Deep down in their hearts they know, as good democrats, that liberty would be fatal to democracy: that a government based upon shifting and irrational opinion must keep it within bounds or run a constant risk of disaster.

They themselves, as a practical matter, advocate only certain narrow kinds of liberty; liberty, that is, for the persons they happen to favor [i.e. groups they want votes from]. *The rights of other persons do not seem to interest them.*

If a law were passed tomorrow taking away the property of a large group of presumably well-to-do persons say, bondholders of the railroads, without compensation and without even colorable reason, they would not oppose it; they would be in favor of it. The liberty to have and hold property is not one they recognize. They believe only in the liberty to envy, hate and loot the man who has it."

- H.L. Mencken

In the end, either candidate would likely be a good President. Or certainly better than the Democrat they will oppose.

Nonetheless, no one politician can solve America's problems. It is not someone in Washington D.C. who will fix the problem. After all, as Reagan said, "*Government is the problem*".

What really matters is that you, the reader, get active in politics. What's the point of state's rights, if the states we return power to are ruled by corrupt officials?

What's the point of local control, if the cities and counties we return power to are run by progressive Democrats because conservatives are "too busy working" and don't desire power so they leave it in the hands of the enemy?

We often look to Presidential candidates for "hope and change", but real change starts with you, in your town. That's the essence of liberty.

One Person Can Change It All

It is often all too easy for conservatives to feel discouraged: the media constantly assaults our beliefs, our opponents are crass and rude, and worse, our victories have been few of late.

Part of it stems from our nature: <u>to be conservative is to be on defense</u>. The problem with being on defense is you will always lose. "The best defense is a good offense" as they say. **In order to truly change things, conservatives have to go on offense**.

It's harder for conservatives, to be sure. Conservatives have jobs and are too busy to be activists, unlike socialists with union jobs that encourage them to take time off for activism or worse, who live off handouts and don't work at all so they have plenty of time to protest for more and more benefits.

One conservative can change it all. <u>YOU</u>. How? Use organizations to pass initiatives.

Initiatives & Referendums

One greatly overlooked path to changing government is through direct action to change your local government. Conservatives often talk about shifting power from the federal to the local governments, yet **unfortunately we've allowed our local governments to be dominated by liberals**. The initiative process is another area where liberals have taken advantage of it, but conservatives neglected it for far too long. We must change that now.

Anything is possible with initiatives: you can propose Amendments to your State's Constitution, require your legislature call for a Constitutional Convention for a Federal Amendment to add Term Limits to Congress, or any other idea no matter how bold. You could even propose your state "gradually and peacefully" declare independence. It is odd how conservatives have never realized the power of the initiative process. We must reclaim that.

If you live in a state that doesn't allow statewide initiatives, you still probably live in a city (i.e. home-rule cities) that allow initiatives.

To understand the problem, you must understand the enemy. Almost all of the corrupt liberal politicians in both parties got their start on the first "rung" of the "political ladder": the mayoral and city council offices.

Even in cities that vote over 70% conservative, there is usually a flaming liberal who is the mayor. How does this happen? Because they have rigged the game.

The first thing they try to do in cities is to make elections "non-partisan". While at first this may sound like a good and noble idea, in reality it has been horrific for conservatives. Only through party primaries can the dishonorable power-hungry politician be held responsible for his bad record or properly vetted by activists.

Worse, when many people get to the voting booth, they have no idea the kind of person they are voting for. By at least having party affiliations, voters won't just be going in blindly to the voting booth.

Allowing partisan elections again will ensure the GOP actually tries to "turn out the vote" for our city elections. They currently don't even pay attention to them in many cities because they have no interest (since they can't run party candidates), and because Democrats already dominate the cities and they haven't bothered to do anything about it.

But the second, more important issue to change in your local city is if they hold their mayoral and city council elections in what is known as an "off year". **It is a downright criminal subversion of the political process**.

In some cities, the City Elections are in Spring 2015, Spring 2017, etc. Why? **To <u>hide</u> elections from the voters or make it a hassle**.

This should be considered criminal fraud.
They are purposefully trying to prevent the
citizenry from voting. This is the true "voter
suppression" going on, but the targets are
conservatives, not minority groups.

In many cities, less than 10% of the
population votes in their mayoral and city
council elections. And holding these elections
pointlessly in Spring 2015 for example, it is
costing many cities millions of dollars!

If conservatives were to lead a mass effort
to merge local elections back onto the
traditional voting date of the first Tuesday in
November of even-numbered years **it would
save us billions of dollars nationally**.

An added bonus is that conservatives would
start taking back the Mayoral and City Council
positions. This helps raise up a new generation
of conservative politicians instead of giving
liberals their first "rung" on the political ladder.

In many cities you will have to research the initiative requirements. Go to ballotpedia.org which conveniently lists the signature requirements and search for your city, or Google if they don't have your city listed. You can contact your city secretary and they will have all the details. Keep any calls friendly so they'll share the info.

But first check to see if your state allows a state-wide initiative. There is no point in just targeting one city when you could get your whole state to require elections be held at their normal time.

I have included a list of all the states that allow initiatives and the number of signatures required. Check with ballotpedia.org for further details. In addition, I have included example wordings of ballot measures. Or just join with the conservatives at governmentalreform.org

They came up with most of these ideas to end corruption in our broken local elections.

Get Active in Your State!

For far too long, conservatives have had their eyes fixed on the never-changing mess in Washington D.C. In order to truly change things, conservatives must focus on their state and local governments where they have greater influence. The average United States Congressman has almost a million constituents, while the average state senator or state congressman has only a few thousand.

Your voice can and will be heard by your local state representatives, your mayor, your city council. Conservatives are for returning power to the states and local governments, so it is of the utmost importance we ensure there is a good government in our states that is worth returning power to.

In order to begin to make a change in your area, it is of the utmost importance that you join the influential groups in your city or county. The most influential groups in almost every part of the United States are the local Chamber of Commerce in each city, the Realtor or Real Estate Associations, and the Police and Firefighter Unions.

The best way to find out who is influencing your area is to look at the mayor of your city's election website (not his/her non-partisan government website), i.e. "Joe for Mayor 2016" for their "endorsements" sections or victory speeches and there you will, unless you have a Tea Party mayor, find a short list of organizations, typically the ones named previously. A simple visit to the political website of your other elected city or county politicians will help you see who put them into power.

One of the most important to join is the Chamber of Commerce, especially if you are a small businessman or in management, as it is important to try to influence your local Chamber to be more socially and fiscally conservative. *I cannot tell you how many times I have spoken with a conservative businessman who yells angrily about the Chamber of Commerce but is not a member.*

Conservatives often sadly separate themselves from the very institutions they need to join to try and change to make them better. Another example would be trade unions.

In most cities, the Chamber of Commerce, Real Estate Associations, Police, Firefighter, and other city worker unions are "kingmakers" that decide who the mayor will be with their powerful lobbies. Without the efforts of conservatives, these groups have a natural vested interest (pay raises) in colluding with the liberal mayors. They are the deciding votes in low-turnout off-year elections.

In fact, the unions are precisely why mayors often try to hold city elections at weird times like spring of odd-years (2015, 2017). And it's why **you, the reader**, should create statewide or citywide initiatives to require local elections be held on the first Tuesday of November of even-numbered years (i.e. 2016, 2018).

But in many of the more conservative parts of the country, conservatives have managed to take over those groups. It can be done. All you have to do is join, influence the members towards conservatism, and be present whenever there are votes. Learn the bylaws of the organizations and try to introduce motions to endorse or support the conservatives in your area.

In many cities, the votes about whether their local Chamber, Association, or Unions endorse the conservative candidate or the RINO establishment candidate (in the primaries) come down to only 1 or 2 votes short for the conservative, especially in smaller towns.

One person can make a difference.

It's also important to remember to become a delegate to your state's Republican convention. Don't under-estimate the power of a delegate: you can submit motions to change the party platform and it is the delegates who have ultimate authority over the party and all of it's candidates. Delegates can propose to do anything with the party they want, whether dissolving it, changing it, setting requirements for candidates, etc.

In theory, it is even possible for delegates to pass "term limits" on their own party at a convention, although many would point out that would give the Democrats an unfair advantage since the GOP would have less incumbents. A better idea may be to require candidates to pass a litmus test, such as approval by the delegates, before getting their nomination.

But for delegates to be effective, they need to work together with the groups in their area to affect change. It has always been conservatives' weak point that we tend to isolate and work independently. Unfortunately, in a Republic it is the side with the numbers that prevails. Conservatives must get out and be active in their area. Simply going to the polls and voting is not enough. Voting is probably the least effective part of politics. A few dozen people in a local tea party often has more effect on politicians than thousands of voters do, because they stick around after the election and hold the politicians accountable.

Similarly, a delegate to the GOP convention can change the party platform, could introduce a litmus test for candidates such as a scorecard which some delegates in Texas tried to pass, as well as whatever other ideas they come up with. Joining conservative groups is the best way to find like-minded conservatives who will join with you and help you change the party and your state.

Conservative Organizations List

The Tea Parties

There are lists of Tea Parties in your local area that can be found online. It is of the utmost importance that you join your local Tea Party chapter and prove to Washington that the Tea Party is alive and kicking!

The Tea Party is the best way to pool many voices into one, and ensure that politicians listen to their constituents and is the first time conservatives have started actually looking at their local state officials, like the mayors and state senators/congressmen who are responsible for half the headache we have! It is urgent that every conservative join their local Tea Party and make a difference locally.

there is a great list of the Tea Party Groups State-by-State here below: www.teaparty911.com/info/locations.htm

Other Effective Conservative Organizations

It is time for conservatives to stop "donating" to politicians who need constant new infusions of cash every election cycle, and start "investing" in conservative causes that will lead to permanent change. One such group, the Governmental Reform Alliance, has been active in advocating for permanent structural change.

They have bold plans where they try to get electoral reform put in place so that conservatives won't have to invest so much time and money each election year just to try to fight back a tidal wave of "progress" forced on them by the liberal media and their cohorts.

The idea is to make permanent changes that will help even the playing field so that conservatives have a fighting chance, such as instituting term limits at the state level, and other measures.

They also try to persuade conservatives, who say that they are all for removing powers from the federal government and restoring them to the state governments, to re-focus on those very state governments they want to put back in control.

For too long, conservatives have allowed liberals and RINOs to dominate those local governments we wish to empower with functions the federal government currently oversees. The goals of the Governmental Reform Alliance, are things we need.

Things like a "None of the Above" on every ballot that actually means something (by defining "None of the Above" as a random citizen of the electorate, it actually has teeth!), a party-wide scorecard rating based on the party platform with consequences for any incumbent who gets an "F", and to ensure that liberals and RINOs in local governments can't just walk all over the people every year like they do now.

There are also many groups doing great things like this in individual states. For a few examples, there are groups such as the Eagle Forums in most states as well as the 9/12 groups and your local Tea Party. In Texas, there are groups such as **TakeoverTexas.org** and **Empower Texans**, who are working hard to affect who Texas elects for their state government. They prefer to focus on the state government and that is precisely what every true conservative should do.

Effective Nationwide Groups

Governmental Reform Alliance
www.governmentalreform.org

Project Veritas (they exposed ACORN)
www.projectveritas.com

FreedomWorks
www.freedomworks.org

Statewide Conservative Groups

Below is a list of some conservative groups that I know of from my days in Texas, Colorado, and California which are doing good work. Please visit and join the groups below as well as the Tea Parties in your area, which are active in your state and helping to elect conservatives to political office in your city, county, and state.

There is a good list of conservative groups at the Governmental Reform Alliance site: governmentalreform.org/organizations.html

Again, there is a great list of the Tea Party Groups State-by-State here below: www.teaparty911.com/info/locations.htm

Please get active with the Tea Party!

Inform them about being delegates and how to censure and kick RINOs off the GOP ballots!

<u>Texas Conservative Organizations</u>

Empower Texans
www.empowertexans.com

Takeover Texas
www.takeovertexas.org

Texas Nationalist Movement
www.thetnm.org

Texas Values
www.txvalues.org

Texas Conservative Coalition
www.txcc.org

Colorado Conservative Organizations

Americans for Prosperity Colorado chapter
http://americansforprosperity.org/colorado/

Reagan Club of Colorado
www.reaganclubco.com

Lincoln Club of Colorado
www.lincolnclubofcolorado.org

Colorado Union of Taxpayers
www.coloradotaxpayer.org

California Conservative Organizations

California Republican Assembly
www.cragop.org

Eagle Forum of California
www.eagleforumofcalifornia.org

Six Californias
www.sixcalifornias.com

If you're in California, there is a "Six Californias" plan that will be on the ballot in 2016. Since California is basically hopeless for the GOP demographically, only this plan to split California into six states has promise, and could re-balance the electoral college.

The Six Californias plan would create new red states to give conservatives there a voice, and mean many of California's electoral votes may go to a GOP candidate, helping re-balance the Presidential races so GOP candidates could have a shot at winning again. Instead of a Democratic President just automatically getting all 55 of California's electoral votes, maybe the GOP could get some of the new states and win 20 of it's electoral votes.

In many states, there are ballot initiative processes that would allow you to do just about anything. Live in Massachusetts and fed up with being ruled by Democrats? Start a ballot initiative to break into two states. Look at the counties Romney won in 2012 to determine what your new state should look like.

Or live in Montana, the Dakotas, Utah, Missouri, or any other state with ballot initiatives and want a Constitutional Amendment for a balanced budget or term limits? Then start collecting signatures!

Or do you live in one of the over 25 states allowing initiatives that had a ban on gay marriage that was overturned by the Supreme Courts by what Scalia called a "judicial coup"? Then start collecting signatures for a state amendment to the constitution to nullify the Supreme Court decision and creating a penalty for any government official who cooperates with the Supreme Court which has "overthrown the Constitution" and which has openly made itself an "domestic enemy" of that very Constitution.

Regardless of what you think of the individual decisions, what matters is the lawless nature of our government. Instead of passing amendments, they just twist it to mean something new. The citizenry must act now or they allow a precedence of lawlessness that is downright dangerous!

Whatever you do, wherever you are, it is of the utmost importance you join the Tea Party and get active with local government!

Be sure to check out the other book by the author, Trevor Smith, which tells the story of up-and-coming star Ben Carson who just might be the person to take on Hillary Clinton or be a great Vice President.

<u>Get it on Amazon at the link below</u>
www.amzn.com/1501012959

Be sure to subscribe to Trevor Smith's Amazon Page by clicking his author name on Amazon when you visit the Ben Carson book above.

Citations and Reference Notes

---

[i] Associated Press. "Democrats remove

state Senate candidate from ballot" *The Washington Times* N.p. 17 March 2015

[ii] Kirby, Brendan. "Insufficiently Republican? State GOP to consider challenges to 18 candidates for office" *AL.com* 17 February 2014

[iii] Lizza, Ryan. "The Revenge of Rand Paul" *The New Yorker* N.p., 6 October 2014